Science and Technology

Crime-Fighting Devices

Robert Snedden

Chicago, Illinois

www.heinemannraintree.com
Visit our website to find out more information about Heinemann-Raintree books.

To order:
☎ Phone 888-454-2279
💻 Visit www.heinemannraintree.com to browse our catalog and order online.

Edited by Andrew Farrow, Adam Miller, and Diyan Leake
Designed by Victoria Allen
Original illustrations © Capstone Global Library Ltd 2012
Illustrated by Oxford Designers and Illustrators
Picture research by Elizabeth Alexander
Originated by Capstone Global Library Ltd
Printed and bound in China by CTPS

15 14 13 12 11
10 9 8 7 6 5 4 3 2 1

Library of Congress Cataloging-in-Publication Data
Snedden, Robert.
  Crime-fighting devices / Robert Snedden.
    p. cm.—(Sci-hi : science and technology)
  Includes bibliographical references and index.
  ISBN 978-1-4109-4275-3 (hc)—ISBN 978-1-4109-4284-5 (pb) 1. Criminal investigation—Technological innovations. 2. Law enforcement—Technological innovations. 3. Crime prevention—Technological innovations. 4. Forensic sciences—Technological innovations. 5. Police—Equipment and supplies. I. Title.
  HV8073.S528 2011
  681'.75—dc22   2010054330

Acknowledgments
The author and publishers are grateful to the following for permission to reproduce copyright material:
Alamy pp. **7 left**, **7 right** (© By Ian Miles-Flashpoint Pictures), **21** (© Chris Deeney), **26** (© les polders), **37** (© JoeFox); Brain Fingerprinting Laboratories, Inc. p. **41**; Corbis pp. 4 (© George Steinmetz), **6**, **31** (© Image Source), **24** (© Luis Carbayo/epa), **27** (© Chad Hunt), **34** (© Surapan Boonthanom/Reuters), **36** (© Michael Reynolds/epa); Getty Images pp. **13** (Alan Thornton), **25** (John Kirk-Anderson); Photolibrary pp. **33**, **35**; Press Association Images pp. **38** (A3471 Boris Roessler/DPA), **39** (Scott Heppell/PA Archive); Rex Features p. **20** (Fraser Spratt); Science Photo Library pp. **10** (Gustoimages), **11** (Sandia National Laboratories), **28** (Mauro Fermariello); Shutterstock pp. **5** (© SVLuma), **12**, **contents page top** (© Kodda), **18** (© Paul Drabot), **19** (© Kletr), **22** (© knotsmaster), **32**, **contents page bottom** (© Gina Sanders), **all background and design features**.

Main cover photograph of a Taser stun gun reproduced with permission of Alamy (© Howard Sayer); inset cover photograph of fingerprint reproduced with permission of shutterstock (© melki76).

The publisher would like to thank literary consultant Nancy Harris and content consultant Suzy Gazlay for their assistance in the preparation of this book.

Every effort has been made to contact copyright holders of material reproduced in this book. Any omissions will be rectified in subsequent printings if notice is given to the publisher.

Disclaimer
All the Internet addresses (URLs) given in this book were valid at the time of going to press. However, due to the dynamic nature of the Internet, some addresses may have changed, or sites may have changed or ceased to exist since publication. While the author and publisher regret any inconvenience this may cause readers, no responsibility for any such changes can be accepted by either the author or the publisher.

Contents

Why do governments use CCTV?

Turn to page 12 to find out!

What is predictive analytics?

Find out on page 32!

Some words are shown in bold, **like this**. These words are explained in the glossary. You will find important information and definitions underlined, <u>like this</u>.

ONE STEP AHEAD

Law enforcement agencies such as police forces must be ready to respond quickly to the threat of crime. There are many ways in which science and technology can help them do this.

A person can be **identified** (found out) from a drop of blood or a single hair. Remote-controlled aircraft watch from above. Special computer programs might even pinpoint crimes before they are committed.

The police can keep an eye on events and spot trouble quickly from command centers like this one.

Fighting crime

People who commit crimes don't want to be caught. They are always trying to find different ways to "get away with it." In many ways the police and **security agencies** like the Federal Bureau of Investigation (FBI) are always trying to keep one step ahead of criminals.

Cyber crime

Computer crime, or **cyber crime**, can involve cracking codes and passwords to break into computer systems. People who do this are called **hackers**. The police need to have computer skills, too, so that they can fight this type of crime. Not all computer hackers are criminals. Many use their talents to help the police. They show them where there might be weaknesses in computer security, for example.

Secret skills

For some tasks, the police and security agencies carefully guard the systems they use. One such task is in dealing with explosive devices. The people who do this are called bomb disposal experts. They keep the methods they use to make bombs safe a secret. Because of this, **terrorists** (people who use violence and threats to achieve aims) and criminals aren't sure what to do to make their bombs more likely to succeed.

Police patrols can be sent swiftly to the scene of a crime.

CRIME PREVENTION

A lot of crime fighting involves preventing crime from happening in the first place. Protecting buildings by using warning systems such as burglar alarms can help to do this. Another way to prevent theft is to mark **property** (belongings) so that it can be easily identified. Thieves are not interested in stealing items that they cannot get rid of easily.

Make sure you have a good, sturdy lock for your bike—and don't forget to use it.

BRIGHT IDEA: SIMPLE STEPS

There are a number of simple steps you can take to protect yourself and your belongings. For example, you should keep valuable objects such as phones and mp3 players safely out of sight. Never leave any of your property unattended in a public place. Make sure doors and windows are closed and locked at night or when you leave the house.

Security sprays

Researchers have developed sprays that contain millions of tiny particles (bits) that are too small to be seen with the naked eye. Each particle carries a code. The code is logged in a police **database** (collection of information). No two particle sprays have the same code. The spray is applied to property and evaporates (turns to a gas). This leaves the particles invisibly behind. Details of the owner of the property are also logged in the police database. If the property is stolen, it can be identified by looking at particles under a microscope.

Another type of spray contains a number of different chemicals. As with the particle spray, no two sprays have exactly the same combination of chemicals. A system can be set up to spray the chemical mixture on **intruders** who enter a building. The spray will remain invisibly on their skin for weeks. It will glow brightly if a special light called **ultraviolet** light is shone on it. If the police find people with the spray on their skin or clothes, they can prove they were at the scene of a crime by identifying the chemical combination of the spray.

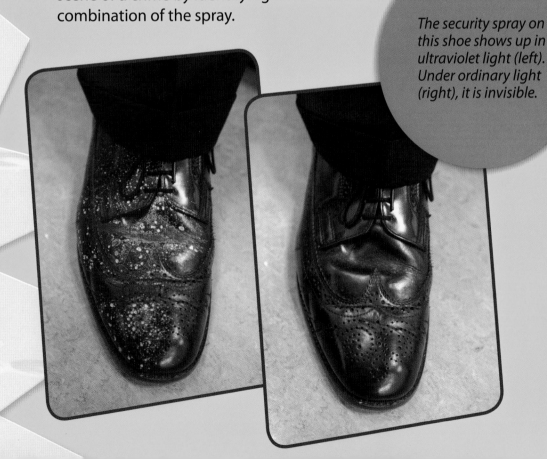

The security spray on this shoe shows up in ultraviolet light (left). Under ordinary light (right), it is invisible.

Intruder alert

Burglar alarms are used to protect homes and other buildings. They are used to send out an alert if an intruder attempts to break in. There are several different kinds of alarms.

Circuit breakers

One of the most basic types of alarm works like a switch in an **electric circuit**. An electric circuit is a path that electricity flows through. A switch is a type of **circuit breaker**. A circuit breaker breaks the flow of electricity around the circuit. For example, a light can be turned on and off by flipping a switch. In the same way, a window or a door can be wired to act like a switch that activates a burglar alarm. One of the easiest ways to do this is to have a small button in the frame of the door or window. When the door is opened, the button is released. This triggers the alarm. These circuit breaker systems are best for stopping people from getting into a building.

Infrared sensors

A warm object, such as a person, gives off **infrared** (heat) energy. Infrared **sensors** in a room are sensitive enough to detect the increase in heat if a person enters. Because infrared light beams are invisible, they can also be used like "tripwires." Rays of infrared light are beamed across the room. If someone moving around the room breaks one of these beams, an alarm is sounded.

Motion sensors

A criminal may find ways to get past a circuit breaker alarm. But there are ways to detect an intruder moving inside a building. <u>Motion sensors are devices that detect movement</u>. Some motion sensors work by sending out bursts of **microwaves** (invisible energy waves). These are reflected back to the sensor from the objects in the room. Anybody moving in the room will get in the way of the reflections. These changes will be detected by the sensor, which will set off an alarm.

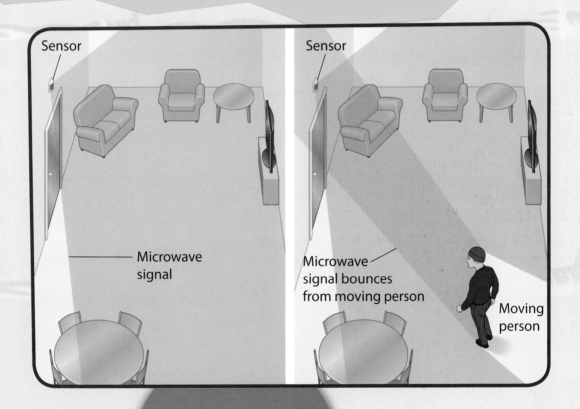

Sensor

Microwave signal

Sensor

Microwave signal bounces from moving person

Moving person

A motion sensor in a room uses invisible microwaves to pick up the movements of an intruder.

Airport security

The police take the threat of a terrorist attack very seriously. Security is very tight at airports in particular. Taking control of an aircraft by force is called **hijacking**. If anything happens to an aircraft when it is in the air, there is very little that anyone on the ground can do to help. **X-ray** machines, metal detectors, and electronic explosive "sniffers" are all used to prevent dangerous items from being taken on board an aircraft.

X-ray machines

As you pass through the departure area of an airport, an X-ray machine examines any bags you have. X-rays are beams that can pass through anything that isn't a metal, or that contains metals. (The calcium in bones is metallic, which is why bones show up in X-rays.) The X-rays help security officers see what is inside every bag. Before baggage goes into the cargo hold of an aircraft, it will be checked for suspicious items. Sometimes a truck carrying an X-ray system is used to scan a whole truckload of baggage.

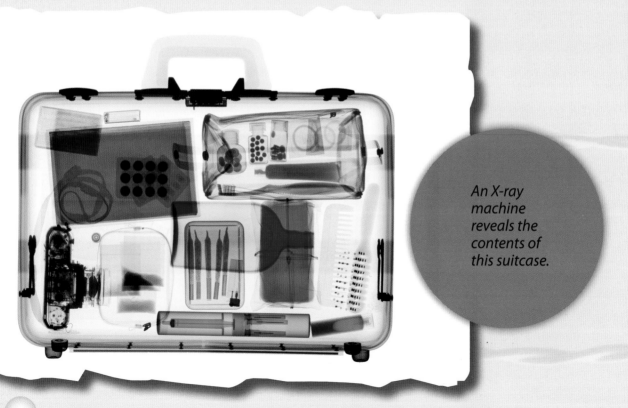

An X-ray machine reveals the contents of this suitcase.

Metal detectors

You will walk through a metal detector while your belongings go through the X-ray machine. The metal detector works by using an **electromagnet**. This is a type of magnet produced by an electric current, or flow of electricity. The current is switched on and off very rapidly. This sends magnetic pulses from one side of the detector to the other. If a metal object, such as a knife, is present, it will get in the way of the magnetic pulses. An alarm will sound.

This device detects chemicals from explosives on a person's skin or clothes.

CANINES VERSUS CHEMICALS

Many airports have machines called **chemical sniffers**. These can detect tiny amounts of the substances used to make bombs. Security officers wipe the fingers of suspected bombers with a special cloth or pad. The chemical sniffer detects any trace of bomb-making chemicals and warns security officers of any possible risk.

So far, however, nothing can outperform the sniffer dog. These specially trained dogs sniff out the faint smells given off by bomb-making chemicals. If the dog smells something suspicious, it will bark and immediately direct its handler to the package or person.

SURVEILLANCE

"**Surveillance**" means **monitoring** (keeping track of) people's activities and gathering information about them. Usually this is done without people knowing about it. Governments and law enforcement agencies use surveillance to give them warnings about possible crimes or terrorist attacks.

CCTV

Closed-circuit television (CCTV) is a very common type of surveillance used in many countries. Video cameras are set up in public places, such as city centers. The images may be monitored on screens in police control centers or by local government officers. Stores may have their own cameras, monitored by their own security.

PRIVACY ISSUES

The United Kingdom is said to have more CCTV cameras per person than any other country. No one knows exactly how many there are. Some people think there may be over four million cameras. This has led many people to worry about their privacy being invaded. Even though they are doing normal, innocent things, they are still being recorded.

CCTV cameras like these monitor activities in towns, cities, and stores. People are often not aware of them.

Smart cameras

The town of East Orange, New Jersey, has been leading the way in monitoring and responding to crime. It is using "smart cameras" that can identify when crimes are taking place. They allow police to respond to an incident very quickly.

The smart cameras can be programmed to recognize the way people behave. For example, if a camera spots one person seeming to threaten another, it issues an alert. An officer at the police department can zoom in on the computer to see if a crime is actually taking place. Meanwhile, another computer program sends the information to a laptop in the police patrol car nearest to the scene. The time from alert to response may be only seconds.

Critics of the cameras point out that it can often be easy for the computer to mistake an innocent act for a criminal one. But, according to the police there, violent crime in East Orange has fallen by more than two-thirds since the smart cameras were introduced.

A CCTV camera has captured the moment a thief steals a woman's handbag.

11:23:20

11:23:25

11:23:30

11:23:31

11:23:32

11:23:33

Facial recognition

If the police are searching for someone in a crowd or on a busy street, they need to be able to pick out the person they are looking for from everyone else. One of the things that help us to tell people apart is that we all have different facial features. Generally speaking, we each have two eyes, a nose, a mouth, and so on. But facial features are all different shapes and distances apart. Facial recognition software breaks up a face's features into measurements called **nodal points**. These can be used to identify someone.

Police forces take photos of the people they arrest. This means they have a huge database containing faces for comparison. Features such as hairstyle or facial hair are ignored, since these can easily be changed. But details such as the distance between the eyes cannot be changed.

How faces are scanned

How people are identified

The grid points are turned into a set of numbers

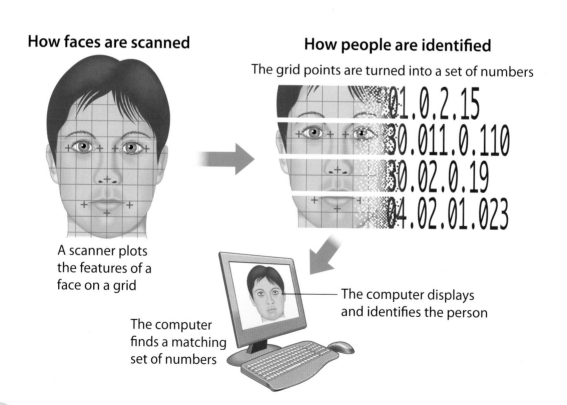

01.0.2.15
30.011.0.110
30.02.0.19
04.02.01.023

A scanner plots the features of a face on a grid

The computer displays and identifies the person

The computer finds a matching set of numbers

Image capture

Facial recognition is different from other forms of identification in an important way. It can be done without any physical contact. An image of a person's face can be captured on camera from a distance, without the person's knowledge.

The captured image can then be analyzed by a computer. The computer looks at the nodal points on the image and attempts to match them to other images held in police files.

A FACE IN THE CROWD

So far, facial recognition systems are not as good at picking out particular faces in a crowd as humans are. The software can compare millions of faces in a second. But it still needs a human to confirm that a match is accurate.

Face app

Police officers in the United States have been fighting crime using smartphones. The police officer can take a picture of a suspect using a facial recognition app (application). This uploads the picture to the police database for identification. If a match is made, the person's identity will appear on the officer's smartphone screen within seconds. Eye scanning and fingerprint recognition apps may also be added. This means that people can very quickly be identified with a high degree of certainty.

Listening in

Sometimes law enforcement agencies keep track of people's activities by listening in on their conversations. There are various devices for doing this.

Bugging the line

Telephone **tapping**, or wire tapping, allows someone to listen in on and record phone conversations. One of the simplest ways of listening in on a telephone is to place a tiny radio **transmitter** (device that sends out signals) inside the phone itself. This device is often called a "bug." The bug sends the telephone calls to a **receiver** hidden nearby. Another way is to attach wires to the telephone line outside. These can be connected to headphones and used to listen to the conversation.

Telephone companies can listen to any call being made. The police and security agencies can request that this be done. But they must have a good reason to believe that monitoring a person's calls may prevent a crime.

Tapping into the telephone wires leading from the building allows a person to listen in on telephone conversations.

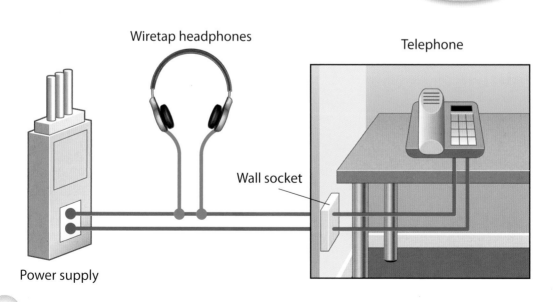

Wiretap headphones

Telephone

Wall socket

Power supply

Cell phones

It is also possible to listen in on cell phone conversations. Cell phones work by sending waves of energy called **radio waves**. With the right equipment, these radio waves can be found and listened to. As with landlines, police may also ask the cell phone company for permission to listen to certain calls.

Laser listening

It is even possible to listen in on a conversation using light. Sounds inside a room cause the glass in windows to vibrate slightly. An invisible beam of light called a **laser** can be pointed at the window from some distance away. A laser is like a very tightly focused beam of light. This beam is reflected back from the window to a laser receiver. The receiver picks up on the tiny vibrations in the window. It changes them into electronic signals, which can be played through a speaker and recorded. It is possible to build both the transmitter and the receiver into something that looks just like an ordinary camera.

A laser listening device can detect tiny vibrations in a window caused by sounds in the room.

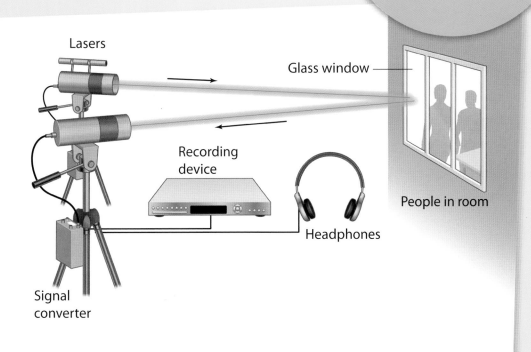

Lasers

Glass window

Recording device

Headphones

People in room

Signal converter

EYES IN THE SKY

One of the most effective pieces of surveillance equipment used by police forces is the helicopter. From high in the air, officers can use cameras and infrared sensors to track suspects.

A helicopter can cover large areas quickly. In 12 minutes, a helicopter can cover an area that would take 50 officers on the ground about 9 hours to search. It can be used to track criminals, search for a missing person, or find an abandoned vehicle. Police officers in the air can check places that are difficult for officers on the ground to reach, such as rooftops or fenced-off areas.

CAMERAS AND SENSORS

A video camera with a powerful zoom lens can be attached under the helicopter's nose. A special mount allows it to swivel in any direction. A high-powered searchlight mounted at the rear of the helicopter can be linked to the video camera. Its beam can be expanded to light up an area the size of a football field. It can also be reduced to pick out a single person running in the darkness.

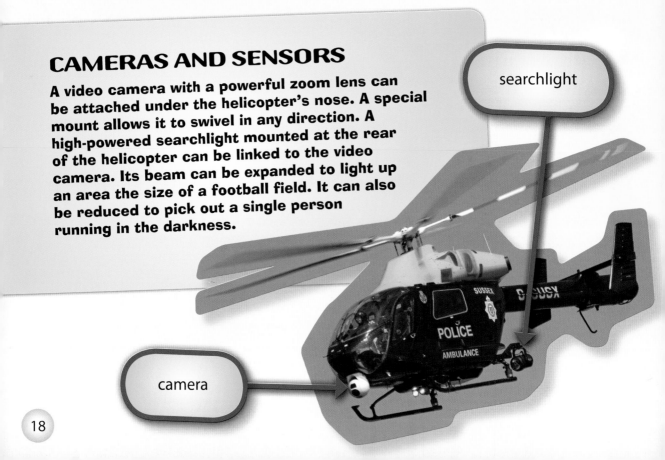

searchlight

camera

Thermal imaging

A **thermal imager** may be placed alongside the camera. This is a device that detects the infrared energy given off by a warm object, such as a hot car engine or a person hiding. The image is displayed on a screen inside the helicopter.

Downlinking

The helicopter crew can use microwave transmitters to send live video pictures to control centers and other police units on the ground. This is called **downlinking**. This view from the air is very useful in providing a "bird's-eye" view of a crime scene.

The officers on board the helicopter can also communicate with people on the ground through a public address system. This can be used in crowd control or to warn people of danger, for example.

A helicopter can be a very quick way to get police officers to where they are needed.

Spy planes

Police forces in several countries have been testing out **unmanned aerial vehicles (UAVs)**. UAVS, also known as **spy drones**, are aircraft piloted by remote control. These spy drones are like the ones used for gathering information in war zones.

In the United States, these spy drones have been used to watch the borders between the United States and Canada and the United States and Mexico. Police forces are pushing to use the drones more, however. They say the drones would be useful in cases such as finding missing children. In the United Kingdom, the government hopes to have a fleet of drones in use when London hosts the Olympic Games in 2012.

An operator on the ground controls a surveillance drone.

Bird's-eye view

Smaller drones can fly at about 1,000 meters (3,280 feet). Larger ones can reach heights of around 6,000 meters (20,000 feet). This makes them invisible from the ground. An operator wearing a pair of video goggles guides small drones from the ground. The goggles are linked to the camera on the spy drone, so the operator sees what the drone sees. The image from the drone can also be transmitted to a laptop screen. Larger drones are programmed to take off and land on their own. They can stay airborne for up to 15 hours.

Voice from above

Aircraft without pilots can also be fitted with speakers, such as the **Long Range Acoustic Device (LRAD)**. The LRAD is a speaker that can produce an intense beam of sound. Like the speakers on a helicopter, it can be used as a loudspeaker to send instructions to people on the ground. It can also produce a sudden burst of deafening noise that is loud enough to force people away. Police used LRAD mounted on ground vehicles to break up protestors at a meeting of world leaders in Pittsburgh, Pennsylvania, in 2009.

Strobe stopper

A spy drone could catch criminals, too, rather than just making them flee. Powerful searchlights, like those on helicopters, could be made to turn into **strobe lights**. These intense, rapidly flashing lights can cause dizziness and loss of balance, stopping criminals in their tracks. This sort of light would be too dangerous to use in a helicopter with pilots, because of the risk of the crew being affected by it. That isn't a problem for a robot drone.

"'Spy planes" like this don't have pilots aboard. They can be used to help catch criminals.

Satellites and Tracking

Police forces make good use of the **Global Positioning System**, or GPS (see box below). It can be used to keep track of officers on foot patrol so they can be found quickly. It is used to track the nearest police car to an emergency and get it there by the quickest route. Police can also track a stolen car using the GPS inside it.

GPS tracking

Vehicle tracking makes use of both GPS and cell phone systems. The GPS pinpoints the vehicle's location. The phone system relays this information to a control center. The GPS can be programmed to send an alert to the owner, or to a security company, if an unauthorized person moves the vehicle.

WHAT IS GPS?

Twenty-four GPS satellites orbit Earth in space. Each one transmits a constant signal, which can be picked up by a GPS receiver. The receiver calculates its distance from each of four different satellites, based on the time it takes for the signals to arrive. It then uses that information to figure out its position on the surface of Earth.

GPS devices can be small enough to fit in a pocket.

BAIT BIKES

Police in many countries have been using GPS-equipped bikes to stop thieves. The bikes, which are deliberately poorly locked, are left in places where bike thefts happen often. Using the hidden GPS trackers, the police can track the gangs behind the thefts. University police on campuses like the University of Wisconsin at Madison are also beginning to use these "bait bikes."

Vehicle tracking devices

Vehicle tracking devices help police to find stolen vehicles. A transmitter is fitted into the car. It can be triggered from a distance if the vehicle is reported as being stolen. It sends out radio signals that can be picked up by a police car or helicopter fitted with a special receiver. The radio signals can be picked up even if the car is hidden in an underground parking lot, for example. The stolen vehicle can quickly be identified through a unique code known only to the police.

GPS and cell phone networks can be used together to track a stolen vehicle.

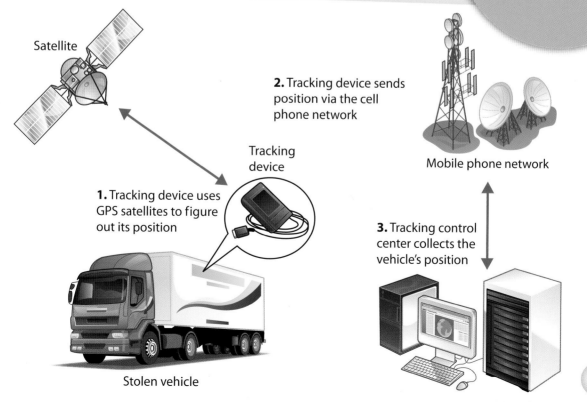

Satellite

2. Tracking device sends position via the cell phone network

Tracking device

Mobile phone network

1. Tracking device uses GPS satellites to figure out its position

3. Tracking control center collects the vehicle's position

Stolen vehicle

THE SCENE OF THE CRIME

After a crime has been committed, it isn't always obvious who did it or how it was done. Detectives use their skills and technology to discover what happened. Investigators will look for a number of clues, such as fingerprints, traces of blood, fibers from clothes, or marks made by tools. They will use these clues to piece together the puzzle and solve the crime.

CSI

Crime Scene Investigators (CSIs) have an important role to play in fighting crime. It is their job to gather **evidence** from the crime scene. This can involve taking photographs of the scene before it is disturbed. For example, the position of an object might be an important clue. They will look for fingerprints, traces of hair or fibers from clothes, and other signs that a criminal might have left behind.

These investigators are gathering evidence at a crime scene in Mexico City, Mexico.

Luminol

Luminol is a substance used by investigators to help find traces of blood. Crime investigators carefully spray luminol over an area where they suspect there may have been blood. If there is any blood, it causes a chemical reaction with the luminol, which creates a blue glow. The amount of blood needed to start the reaction is very small. Luminol will even reveal where attempts have been made to remove bloodstains. The blue glow only lasts for about 30 seconds. But this is enough time for the investigators to take photographs that can be used as evidence.

Luminol has been used to reveal that the person who made this footprint has stepped in blood.

If the shoe fits ...

Photographs of shoeprints or tire tracks left at a crime scene can be sent from a crime scene straight to a database. Here they will be analyzed and matched with thousands of other shoeprints and tracks. Shoeprints can help link someone to a crime scene. If a suspect is arrested, his or her shoes can be checked to see if they match the prints that have been found. Unlike a fingerprint, a shoeprint isn't proof without doubt. But it helps the detectives to build their case.

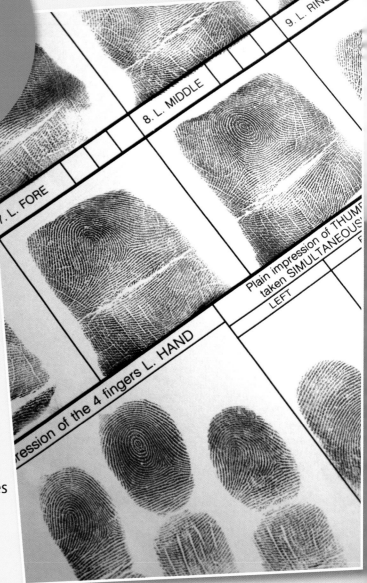

Fingerprints

Searching for fingerprints at a crime scene has long been a trusted method of identifying who has been present. <u>There are two types of fingerprint</u>. Visible prints are those left imprinted in a soft material, like a bloodstain or fresh paint. **Latent** prints are the ones that are made when oils on the skin are left behind after touching a surface. This makes a copy of the fingerprints. Latent prints are usually invisible to the naked eye.

Seeing fingerprints

The oldest—and still the most used—method of making latent prints visible is to dust the surface of an object with a powder. The powder sticks to the oils in the print, so it can be seen. The investigator can then photograph the print or take a copy of it by carefully pressing sticky tape over the powder. Another way to look for prints is by using a laser beam. Latent prints will become visible when the light from a laser shines on them.

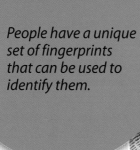

Database search

Once the fingerprints have been taken, they can be compared against a database of fingerprints to see if there is a match. In the past this was done by eye. This could take up to two weeks to carry out. Today, computer software can come up with a match in around 20 minutes.

Fingerprint scanners

Police can now use cell phone-sized fingerprint scanners to check the identity of suspects instantly. The scanners can also be used to help identify murder **victims**. The index finger is scanned. The file is then transmitted through a computer or cell phone to the central fingerprint database, where it is checked.

BIOMETRICS

If you look closely at your fingertips, you will see a pattern of lines. This pattern is different for everyone. Even identical twins have different prints. Your fingerprints stay the same throughout your life. This means that fingerprints can be used to identify a person. The study of the ways in which people differ from each other according to their body characteristics is called biometrics.

This is a portable fingerprint scanner used by troops in Afghanistan. Police forces use similar models.

Place left thumb on the fingerprint sensor

DNA profiling

There is a type of code that is found in all living things. That code is **DNA**. It carries the instructions for building and maintaining a new living thing. <u>DNA is passed on from one generation to the next. Each person has a different DNA code from every other person</u>. This means that everyone has a different DNA **profile** (set of information used for identification). Every part of the body contains this DNA profile. The smallest skin flake left behind at a crime scene can be used to find the DNA profile of a suspect.

Building a profile

A tiny amount of DNA from a drop of blood, a single hair, or a flake of skin from a fingerprint can be grown into a larger sample. This sample can be examined and used to create a profile.

This scientist is comparing DNA profiles in a laboratory.

DNA databases

Scientists can examine a DNA profile and compare it with a sample taken from a suspect or with the samples already in a DNA database. If police scientists find a match, they can be certain that there is less than a one in one billion chance that the samples came from different people. But if there is no match, the investigators can be sure that the person they suspected is innocent.

Contamination

The equipment used to create a DNA profile is very sensitive. Investigators have to be very careful to make sure that samples are not contaminated (mixed with unwanted substances). If their own, or anyone else's, DNA gets into a sample, the results are worthless. Full protective clothing, including face masks, is worn when the sample is being taken from the crime scene. It is also worn when the sample is being examined in the laboratory.

CRIME AND COMPUTERS

As more and more of our activities take place online, the Internet has become a target for criminals. Police forces cannot do much to trace those who use computers to carry out crimes. Often the police will find that the criminals are based in other countries. This makes it difficult to bring them to justice.

International crime

Because the Internet spans the world, it means that criminals using it can operate on an international basis. It is possible for criminals in one country to gain access to people's bank accounts in another country.

Being vigilant

We all have to be smart about protecting our personal details while online. Security software, **antivirus software**, and computer **firewalls** can all help to prevent an outsider from getting access to and damaging a computer. These protections should all be kept up-to-date and used to their full advantage.

Types of fraud

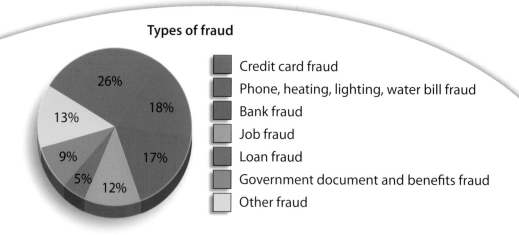

26%
18%
13%
9%
17%
5%
12%

Credit card fraud
Phone, heating, lighting, water bill fraud
Bank fraud
Job fraud
Loan fraud
Government document and benefits fraud
Other fraud

Piracy

One of the biggest computer crimes is that of **piracy**. This is the illegal copying, using, and selling of things such as music, DVDs, computer games, and software. There are many different ways to stop this from happening. For example, computer software comes with a unique code that must be entered before the software can be used.

Skimming

Skimming is when identity thieves try to get the details of a person's bank card. One way of doing this is to fit a false panel onto a bank **ATM** (automated teller, or cash, machine). A tiny camera hidden inside the ATM records the personal identification number (PIN) entered by the card owner. At the same time, a device called a skimmer reads the magnetic strip on the back of the card. If thieves get hold of this information, they can make a copy of the card and use it to take out cash or buy goods.

The police have created an anti-skimming device. It is placed invisibly behind the ATM screen beside the real card reader. If it detects a skimmer in operation, it can prevent it from working. It can also detect illegal devices, such as cameras, attached to the ATM.

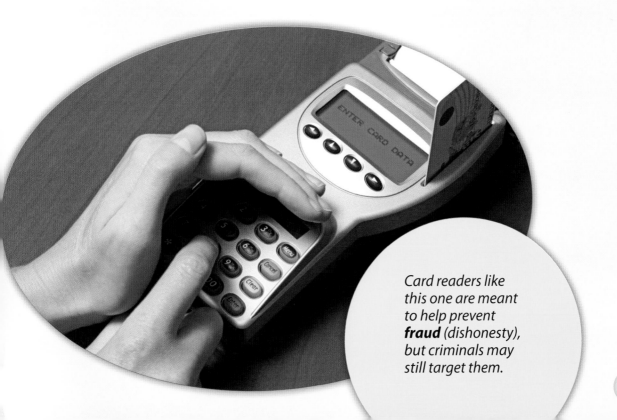

*Card readers like this one are meant to help prevent **fraud** (dishonesty), but criminals may still target them.*

Future crime

The police can use the powerful database and analysis tools of the computer to fight crime. In 2010 some police forces even began trying to predict crimes before they happened.

Predictive analytics

Using powerful computer software, police information technology experts combined lots of information. This included past crimes, known behavior patterns of offenders, surveillance information, reports of crimes, and even the weather. The software uses all of this information to predict where crimes are most likely to take place.

The science that allows these predictions to be made is called **predictive analytics**. The IBM computer company has developed the software. When it was tested in Memphis, Tennessee, crime rates fell by nearly one-third. In Florida, the Department of Justice used the software to predict which young offenders (criminals under the age of 18) were most likely to go on to become adult criminals.

As a result of a crime like this, police might learn that this offender is likely to commit similar crimes in the future.

Repeat offenders

Police officers can use predictive analytics to pinpoint which prisoners are likely to commit further crimes when they are released from prison. Various factors such as education, lifestyle, family relationships, and drug use are all taken into account. The idea is that people picked out by the computer as likely offenders can be given the help they need to avoid crime in the future.

BRIGHT IDEA?

Professor Richard Berk of the University of Pennsylvania developed predictive analytics software. It takes more than 20 different factors into account in making its predictions. In some cases, these predictions have proved to be very accurate.

But some people are worried about predictive analytics. They say that it means people could be judged for something that they haven't actually done—just something they might do. If the results are wrong, it could mean someone being accused for just thinking about committing a crime!

Police officers make full use of the power of computers in fighting crime.

DEALING WITH DANGER

One of the most dangerous jobs in the fight against crime and terrorism is dealing with explosive devices such as bombs. Highly trained squads carry out this work. These squads can be made up of police officers or members of the armed forces, like an army.

Remote control

How experts set about tackling a bomb will depend on a number of things, such as the type of device and its position. If possible, the bomb disposal team will try to deal with the bomb from a distance. They have a number of long-range devices to help them in their work.

The Wheelbarrow

The bomb disposal team may use a device called the Wheelbarrow. It is controlled remotely. The operator can send it into a dangerous situation without endangering himself or herself.

Remote-controlled devices like this allow bomb disposal experts to examine bombs as safely as possible.

Getting around

The Wheelbarrow runs on a "caterpillar track," like the ones found on bulldozers and tanks. It allows the Wheelbarrow to move easily over rough ground. The Wheelbarrow can even climb up stairs on its track. It has an extendible arm that can rotate in a full circle. The arm can be fitted with equipment such as cameras and chemical sensors. The operator uses these to build up a picture of the bomb.

Hands-on heroes

When a bomb cannot be dealt with remotely, bomb technicians must approach it directly. They put on heavily **armored** protection suits made of a material similar to that used in bulletproof vests. The suit protects all parts of the body, but this restricts movement. It also cuts down on how easily technicians can see their surroundings. So, while offering protection, it also makes technicians' jobs a little harder.

Bomb suits contain cooling systems, so technicians do not overheat inside the heavy suit. They also have built-in radio communications. These allow technicians to report on their progress in making the bomb safe.

A bomb technician wears full protective gear.

Staying safe

Sometimes police officers may find themselves in dangerous situations. In these circumstances, there are various items of protective clothing and other equipment they can use to help reduce the risk of injury.

Riot shields

Police riot shields give protection from objects thrown during large-scale disturbances. They are made of strong, clear plastic and come in a variety of sizes. They range from full body length to smaller, round shields.

Shields and visors protect officers in crowd-control situations.

Stab-proof vests

Being attacked by someone armed with a knife is one of the hazards a police officer may face. Wearing a stab-proof vest gives some protection. The vest has a very tightly woven fabric made of heavy nylon. It takes a great deal of force to push a knife through it. It means that the officer is much less likely to be seriously injured.

Bulletproof vest

A bulletproof vest is designed to protect the wearer from gunshot wounds. There are two types: soft vests and rigid vests. Like stab-proof vests, soft vests are made of a tightly woven fabric. This fabric is made of a very strong, but flexible, material called **Kevlar**. It allows the wearer to move around normally and spreads the force of a bullet's impact across the tight weave of the vest. This means there is not enough force left for the bullet to seriously injure the officer. Soft vests are effective against handguns. But they may not stop a high-powered rifle bullet, which travels faster than one from a handgun.

Body armor

Rigid vests are like the armor worn by knights in the past. Instead of being made of metal, however, they are made of a tough, light material. Bullets simply bounce off a rigid vest. But it is not so easy to move around while wearing one. A bulletproof vest doesn't prevent all injury. The bullet might not pierce the skin, but the force of impact will still leave severe and painful bruising.

A stab-proof vest like this protects a police officer from knife attack.

Fighting back

Police officers need some way to fight back and defend themselves. Although weapons such as handguns may be used in extreme circumstances, there are other options that are less deadly.

For example, there are shotguns that can fire non-deadly **ammunition** such as a bean-bag round. The "bean bag" is a small fabric sack filled with small balls of lead. When it is fired from the shotgun, the sack spreads out as it flies through the air. It delivers a heavy blow on impact. It is a short-range weapon and is accurate up to 12 meters (40 feet).

Flash-Ball

Special units of the French police force use the Flash-Ball gun. It looks like a large double-barreled handgun. It can be used to fire a variety of ammunition, such as **tear gas** or a soft rubber ball. It is possible to have different types of ammunition in each barrel. According to the manufacturers of the Flash-Ball, being struck by the rubber ball is like being punched by a professional boxer!

A French police officer gets ready to fire a tear gas gun at rioters.

Water cannon

One very effective way of breaking up a crowd of rioters is to use a water cannon. The water cannon is mounted on a truck and can shoot a high-pressure jet of water a distance of 40 to 60 meters (140 to 200 feet). The truck holds about 8,000 liters (1,800 gallons) of water. The operator can safely direct the cannon from inside the truck.

Electroshock

Electroshock weapons work by giving an electric shock that can stun a person. The shock also makes them lose control of their muscles for a short time. The Taser is one such weapon. It fires two darts, which stay connected to the gun by long, thin wires. The darts and wires are held in a case called a cartridge. The cartridge is replaced after each use. The main body of the gun holds the batteries that send the electric charge through the wires. It has a maximum range of around 10 meters (35 feet).

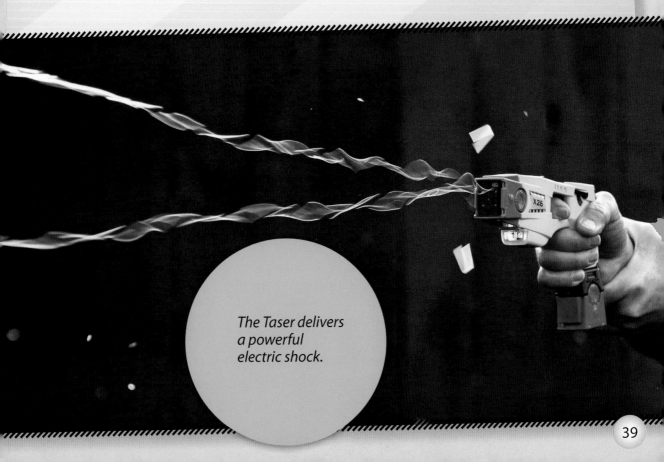

The Taser delivers a powerful electric shock.

FUTURE TECHNOLOGY

Some researchers imagine a time when much police work will be carried out by robots. How close is this to becoming a reality? Police in the United States recently borrowed a special robot from NASA, the U.S. space agency, to help them in a hunt for evidence to a crime. The following story shows how it was used.

Buried evidence

In 1991 Dawn Sanchez was killed. Both the gun used to kill her and the car in which she was last seen could not be found. Due to this important lack of evidence, the man suspected of the crime could not be charged with her murder.

Almost 20 years later, someone informed the police that the car had been taken apart and buried in a large abandoned lot in Alviso, California. The problem was that the exact location of the car was unknown. Also, there were far too many other pieces of junk metal buried there to make a search with metal detectors possible.

Calling NASA

The police turned for help to the experts at the United States Geological Survey (USGS), who in turn called on the scientists at NASA. They had been working on magnetic and **ground-penetrating radar** sensors. Ground-penetrating radar uses microwaves to "see" beneath the ground. Under ideal conditions it can reveal things up to 15 meters (50 feet) below the surface. NASA uses sensors like this mounted on small air and ground robots as part of their Earth science investigations.

Together, a team of computer software experts and scientists from NASA and USGS took a robot equipped with sensors to the abandoned lot.

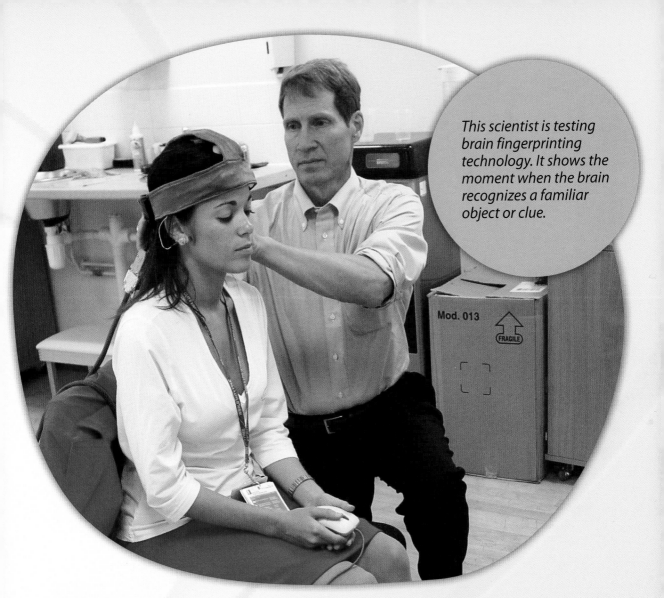

This scientist is testing brain fingerprinting technology. It shows the moment when the brain recognizes a familiar object or clue.

Robot justice

The rover (robot) used its sensors to check out the area. The map it built up was analyzed by the software experts. They were able to pinpoint the most likely locations for the buried car. Following the experts' recommendations, the police began to dig. They found car parts that matched the suspect's car.

Faced with this evidence in court in August 2009, Bernardo Bass was found guilty of **manslaughter** (killing without meaning to). This was 18 years after the crime was committed. Once again, advanced technology had come to the aid of the police.

TIMELINE

3000 BCE
One of the earliest police forces was created in Egypt. The pharaoh (Egyptian ruler) gave several people the job of providing justice (fairness) and security in the country. The chief of police for each district had the title *sab heri seker*, which means "chief of the hitters."

7 BCE
Policing used to be looked on as a very low-ranking job. The ancient Greeks and Romans used slaves, and even some former criminals, as police. In 7 BCE the emperor Augustus created an organized police force in Rome. It was also responsible for dealing with fires.

5th–11th centuries CE
In Anglo-Saxon England, all adult males were responsible for each other's good behavior. If a crime was seen to take place, everyone was expected to raise an alarm, called a "hue and cry," and chase after the criminal. Areas of the country, called shires, were led by a shire-reeve. This is where the word *sheriff* comes from.

1789
Shortly after the Revolutionary War (1775–83), in the United States the Judiciary Act created the role of marshalls. Each of the 13 original states had a marshall, who was in charge of upholding national laws. Each marshall had deputies under him who carried out local law enforcement.

1829
The London Metropolitan Police Department came into being. The Metropolitan Police became a model for police forces across Britain, the United States, and elsewhere in the world.

1865
The U.S. Secret Service was set up to fight counterfeiting—the illegal printing of money. Early on, its role also included protecting national security—duties that later passed on to the FBI and other groups. Since 1901 the Secret Service has had the role of guarding the president of the United States. Its duties also include protecting other political figures and their families.

1908
The Federal Bureau of Investigation (FBI) was formed in the United States. Still in place today, its job is to enforce criminal laws and protect the country from outside attacks.

2002
In response to the terrorist attacks of September 11, 2001, the Department of Homeland Security was formed. Its job is to protect the United States against terrorist attacks and to respond to natural disasters like hurricanes.

1844
The New York City Police Department (NYPD) was established. It and the Boston Police Department are considered by many to be the first "modern" police departments in the United States.

1923
Interpol was founded by the police chief of Vienna, Austria. Today, over 180 member countries share information about criminal activities and help each other with arrests.

1947
As part of the National Security Act, the Central Intelligence Agency (CIA) was formed in the United States. Still in place today, its job is to monitor issues related to national security.

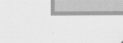

Glossary

ammunition things fired from a gun, such as bullets or shells

antivirus software software designed to prevent harmful viruses from working on a computer

armored covered by armor, a hard, protective covering

ATM (automated teller machine) type of computer usually found beside a bank. It allows people to take money from their accounts.

biometrics study of the ways in which people differ from each other according to their body characteristics

chemical sniffer machine that can detect tiny amounts of materials used to make bombs

circuit breaker device that breaks the flow of electricity around a circuit

closed-circuit television (CCTV) type of surveillance in which video cameras are set up in public places. The images can be monitored by police or security officers.

Crime Scene Investigator (CSI) name given to a police officer who looks for evidence at the scene of a crime

cyber crime computer crime, such as hacking

database collection of information gathered together so that different items can be easily sorted and found

DNA part of cells that carries the information needed for making and maintaining a living thing

downlinking when a helicopter crew uses microwave transmitters to send live pictures to control centers and officers

electric circuit path for electricity to flow through

electromagnet type of magnet that works when electricity flows through a coil of wire

evidence something used to prove that something has happened

firewall type of software protection for computers that stops other people from getting access to the computer on a network

fraud deliberately deceiving someone in order to gain an unlawful benefit

Global Positioning System (GPS) system of satellites that tracks the exact position of a person or thing

ground-penetrating radar system that uses microwaves to "see" beneath the ground

hacker person who cracks codes and passwords to break into a computer system

hijack take over an airplane by force

identify establish the identity of a person, to recognize him or her

infrared type of energy that it is invisible to our eyes, but that we can feel as heat

intruder someone who enters a home or building without permission

Kevlar type of very strong yet light fiber; it is five times stronger than steel, but very flexible

laser high-energy, tightly focused beam of light

latent something (for example, a fingerprint) that is there but cannot be seen

law enforcement agency branch of government whose job it is to enforce laws—for example, the police

Long Range Acoustic Device (LRAD) speaker that can produce an intense beam of sound

luminol substance used by investigators to find traces of blood

manslaughter kill someone without meaning to

microwave short type of energy wave that can be used to send information

monitor watch, keep track of, or check

nodal point distinguishing feature of the face

piracy illegal copying, using, and selling of things such as music and software

predictive analytics way of analyzing information and using it to try to predict the future

profile set of information used for identification

property personal belongings

radio wave energy wave that can send signals through the air without using wires

receiver something for detecting energy waves such as microwaves or radio waves sent by a transmitter

satellite object that travels around a larger object in space, such as a weather satellite going around Earth

security agency government institution that provides secret intelligence, such as the FBI

sensor something that detects something, such as light or sound

skimming when identity thieves try to get the details of a person's bank card

spy drone aircraft powered by remote control that is used to gather information

strobe light device that produces a very bright, flashing light

surveillance keeping a close watch on someone

tapping technique that allows someone to listen in on and record telephone conversations

tear gas gas that causes a burning sensation in the eyes, often used to control crowds

terrorist someone who uses violence and threats to achieve his or her aims

thermal imager device that detects heat and displays it on a screen

transmitter something that sends a signal, usually in the form of radio or other energy waves

ultraviolet special kind of light that can make some chemicals show up

unmanned aerial vehicle (UAV) *see* spy drone

victim person who is harmed as the result of criminal activities

X-ray beam that can pass through anything that isn't metal or that contains metal

Find Out More

Books

Beck, Esther. *Cool Crime Scene Basics: Securing the Scene*. Edina, Minn.: ABDO, 2009.

Graham, Ian. *Why Science Matters: Fighting Crime*. Chicago: Heinemann Library, 2009.

Gray, Leon. *Solve That Crime!: Virtual Crime: Solving Cybercrime*. Berkeley Heights, N.J.: Enslow, 2009.

Harris, Nathaniel. *Pros and Cons: Crime Fighting*. Pleasantville, N.Y.: Gareth Stevens, 2010.

Jeffrey, Gary. *Graphic Forensic Science: Solving Crimes with Trace Evidence*. New York: Rosen Central, 2008.

Rose, Malcolm. *Scene of the Crime*. New York: Kingfisher, 2008.

Websites

www.fbi.gov/fbikids.htm
The Federal Bureau of Investigation's kids' page contains games and stories to help young people learn about the work of the FBI.

www.dnai.org/d/index.html
Learn more about DNA profiling.

www.justice.gov/criminal/cybercrime/rules/kidinternet.htm
Learn more about avoiding cyber crime.

www.mcgruff.org
This gives advice about staying safe and preventing crime, from McGruff the Crimefighting Dog (a National Crime Prevention Council website).

www.cia.gov/kids-page/index.html
Learn more about the Central Intelligence Agency (CIA) at this website.

Topics to research

Computer security
Do you have personal information on a computer? What are the best ways to ensure that this is kept safe?

Shed some ultraviolet light on the subject
Find out whether security marker pens are available in your local stores. They contain ink that is only visible under ultraviolet light. Think about any items you might want to mark so that they could be identified as yours if they were stolen.

Homeland Security
The Department of Homeland Security was created in 2002 to deal with the threat of terrorism in the United States. Find out more about what it does.

Predictive analytics
Check out the arguments for and against predictive analytics. What are your own conclusions about using it as a way to reduce crime?

Index